DECOUPAGE
The Big Picture Sourcebook

Edited and Introduced by
Eleanor Hasbrouck Rawlings

Dover Publications, Inc., New York

Published in Canada by General Publishing Company, Ltd., 30 Lesmill Road, Don Mills, Toronto, Ontario.
Published in the United Kingdom by Constable and Company, Ltd., 10 Orange Street, London WC 2.

Decoupage: The Big Picture Sourcebook is a new work, first published by Dover Publications, Inc., in 1975.

DOVER *Pictorial Archive* SERIES

Decoupage: The Big Picture Sourcebook belongs to the Dover Pictorial Archive Series. Up to ten illustrations from this book may be reproduced on any one project or in any single publication free and without special permission. Wherever possible please include a credit line indicating the title of this book, author and publisher. Please address the publisher for permission to make more extensive use of illustrations in this book than that authorized above.
The republication of this book in whole is prohibited.

International Standard Book Number: 0-486-23182-8
Library of Congress Catalog Card Number: 75-11080

Manufactured in the United States of America
Dover Publications, Inc.
180 Varick Street
New York, N. Y. 10014

INTRODUCTION

Decoupage—the art of decorating objects with paper cutouts—was originated by seventeenth-century Venetian cabinetmakers. They conceived the idea of cutting out hand-colored prints or engravings, gluing them onto various pieces of furniture and submerging these designs under many coats of lacquer. Originally decoupage was devised as a means of helping to meet the demand for the elaborately painted and gilded ("japanned") furniture then in vogue. By the eighteenth century, the art of decoupage had become popular all over Europe and in England. It was a favorite pastime of the nobility and created a lively business for cabinetmakers, artists and printers.

London in the 1760's was the world of King George III and William Pitt. It was the world of Samuel Johnson and his Boswell, of David Garrick, of Sir Joshua Reynolds and William Hogarth. It was also the world of Robert Sayer, a printer, who produced a book in 1762 titled *The Ladies Amusement, or the Whole Art of Japanning Made Easy*. Several pages of instruction were followed by 200 pages containing 1500 designs from copperplates. Animals, birds, borders, flowers, fruits, garlands, insects, pastoral scenes and chinoiserie were rendered in black and white to be hand colored. This book has been ever since a source for design in many fields—textiles, wallpaper, porcelain, silver and needlework as well as decoupage.

In presenting a book of designs for decoupage in 1975 Dover Publications makes available a new selection from its extensive archives. Some of the motifs in this collection are from volumes that are hundreds of years old; some are by artists whose names have been forgotten.

In compiling this anthology an effort has been made to cover as wide a range of subjects as possible, sometimes following the lead of *The Ladies Amuse-ment,* but exploring some new channels of interest as well. Masculine as well as feminine tastes are represented; stylized as well as realistic designs have been selected. To provide the elements of symmetry, mirror images and repeats are also supplied.

Some of the designs in this book can be applied "as is" to the object to be decorated; others should be cut apart, edited and reassembled. Within the limits of artistic compatibility one can delete, augment, combine and rearrange as imaginatively as one wishes. In fact, according to Mr. Hiram Manning of Boston, the teacher and mentor of so many *découpeurs* in twentieth-century America, the creative use of the raw picture material is an essential element of true decoupage.

Before the development of color printing, all designs for decoupage were colored by hand. Even today most serious *découpeurs* prefer to do their own coloring; they use their skill not only to color a black-and-white print to their own taste, but also to accent or tone down a precolored design. The full-color designs reproduced here can be used immediately as cutouts or can serve as examples of coloring for black-and-white prints.

Most of the designs are reproduced in soft gray-black on white, to be hand colored as were those of *The Ladies Amusement*. The precise detail and shading in these designs will enrich any palette in which they are rendered. The paper on which they are printed takes oil-color pencils well and—being quite thin—requires fewer coats of varnish to bury the prints than would thicker paper, which should be peeled or sanded before use.

There are many sources for good prints today in addition to the Dover Publications Pictorial Archive. Greeting cards, wrapping paper, old books, programs, etc., offer an endless supply. Studios of decoupage have fine collections, acquired over many years; a few are listed at the end of this Introduction.

Avoid photographs, prints with shiny surfaces, and those from newspapers with printing on the reverse side, because the printing on the back eventually surfaces, and all your work is destroyed.

SUGGESTIONS FOR DECOUPAGE PROJECTS

Articles of wood, metal, glass, ceramic and even plastic can be decoupaged. You can choose an heirloom as small as a stamp box or a masterpiece as large as a grand piano. Here is a list of suggestions.

> Boxes of all shapes and sizes—wood, tin, ceramic, papier maché
> Trays—wood, tin, papier maché
> Furniture—from small tables to tall secretaries
> Mirrors, waste baskets, napkin rings, hand mirrors, picture frames
> Door frames, wall panels, screens, plaques, mantels
> Lamps, shades, urns, vases, ash trays, ornamental plates
> Basket purses, box purses, picnic baskets, mail boxes
> Desk accessories, album covers, book ends, câche pots, paperweights
> Christmas tree ornaments, jewelry, eggs (natural and artificial)
> Wig stands, driftwood, weathered wood, etc., etc.

If it has a surface you probably can decoupage it!

After selecting an object to be decorated and working out a design, one next colors and seals the print or prints. Do not cut out a design until after you have finished coloring and sealing it.

COLORING AND SEALING YOUR PRINTS

Good-quality colored pencils with an oil base are the most satisfactory medium for coloring prints. They are easy to manage, blend well, and can be erased with a hard pink eraser.

Materials
> Oil-base colored pencils (Prismacolor, Derwent or Colorama). Two shades of each primary and secondary color, black, white, terra cotta, yellow ochre, burnt umber, pink, flesh, slate gray. Some extra colors you may wish to add are emerald green, fuchsia, cerise, scarlet lake, madder red, turquoise blue, lemon yellow, indigo and burnt carmine.
> Pencil sharpener.
> Pink eraser.
> Sealer solution. (Be economical and prepare this yourself by mixing equal parts of white shellac and denatured alcohol.)
> Inexpensive ½″ brush.

A Review of Color Theory

Yellow, blue and red are *primary colors.*
Green, violet and orange are *secondary colors*—

mixed from the primary colors.

Yellow-green, blue-green, blue-violet, red-violet, red-orange, yellow-orange and all their variants are *tertiary colors*—mixed from the primary and secondary colors.

Black, white and gray are *neutral.*

Raw umber, burnt umber, raw and burnt siennas, the ochres and black are *earth colors.*

Colors differ in three ways:
Hue—whether it is, for example, red or green.
Value—whether it is a light or dark shade.
Intensity—whether it is brilliant or grayed.

Warm colors are those that are predominantly red and yellow.
Cool colors are those that are predominantly blue and green.

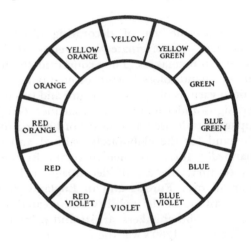

The Color Spectrum

A subtle balance of all these qualities is essential for a harmonious effect. Unless you have had experience with colors, use brilliant ones in smaller areas for accent, with two or three other hues and values for larger areas. Or borrow a scheme from another source: it might be a plate (Creil, faience, Delft, Famille Rose, Gaudy Welsh), a chintz, a wallpaper, a picture in a book or any other object you happen upon. The important point is to choose a color scheme that you like and to stick to it.

Here are a few academic color schemes, which should not be followed too literally.

Monocromatic. Several shades of one hue. Mix with white to produce paler shades; mix with raw umber for darker shades. Don't use black to darken shades; it deadens color. The popular *Toile de Jouy* wallpaper and fabric patterns are printed in monochromatic color schemes. *Grisaille* is also monochromatic, being done in black, gray and white in various combinations. This gives a marble-like effect under varnish.

Analogous. Colors adjacent to each other on the spectrum are harmonious and will blend well. Examples: Red-orange, orange, yellow-orange; or violet, blue-violet, blue; or blue-green, green, yellow-green; or raw umber, terra cotta, burnt sienna, burnt ochre.

Complementary. Colors opposite on the spectrum; mixed in equal portions they produce gray. If complementaries are used together in a print, blend a bit of the cool color into its warm complement, or vice versa. If one of the two hues is grayed, the pair will be more compatible. Examples: red and green; blue-violet and yellow-orange; red-orange and blue-green.

Split Complementary. A color and those adjacent to its complement. Again, tone down the warm colors by blending a little of the cool complement into it. Examples: blue, yellow-orange and red-orange; or yellow, blue-violet and red-violet.

Triad. Three colors equidistant on the spectrum. Examples: red, yellow, blue; or green, orange, violet.

Coloring Techniques

A magazine resting on a tabletop is a firm enough surface on which to color and is not *too* hard, as bare wood or glass would be. Too hard a surface will make your coloring look scratchy.

If a print is too dark, erase it partially with a good pink eraser so that it will take the color better.

For decoupage under glass, pastel or subdued colors may be used; but use stronger hues if the object is to be varnished, because many coats of varnish markedly tone down all color.

Always, *always* work with sharp pencils.

Follow the shading lines on the print for direction of pencil strokes and density of color. Use short uneven strokes—parallel and close, close together—rather than long ones—to fill in areas. Long strokes have a way of not covering as evenly as short ones.

Use light strokes to begin with and stay within the boundary lines, or colors and detail will become smeared and muddy.

Start with the darkest color in the most heavily shaded area at the outside contours of your print. Blend a lighter tone slightly over the darker tone, gradually working into the lighter shaded area, and then continue on toward the center of the section to be colored. *Don't* cover up all of the white!

Some examples of starting with darkest tones and gradually lightening them:

    for skin: brown, terra cotta, pink, flesh
    for scrolls: brown, burnt umber, burnt ochre, yellow ochre
    for garments: violet, fuchsia, pink; or violet, ultramarine blue, sky blue

    for leaves and stems: brown, dark green, apple green, lemon yellow
    for bark: brown, terra cotta, pink.

Use colored pencils to thicken stems or lines in your print that are too thin to cut.

Leave white highlights on the parts of the design nearest you, i.e., the folds of the garment, the forward curl of the scroll. Sometimes the highlight should be on the side where the light is coming from. This adds an illusion of depth and an inner glow under varnish.

Always blend your colors with your white pencil, following the contours of the design; then accent tiny bits of detail, deep shadow and mere suggestions of outlines, here and there, with a needle-pointed black pencil, or a dark shade of the color on the design. Raw umber and burnt carmine are useful for fine detail also.

Do not color the nose on a face; it is an all-important highlight. Pick up lips, hair, eyes and complexions with appropriate colors, but delicately. A light touch is all-important here. Remember that a bore is a person who tells you everything. Experiment a little, practice a great deal and don't forget that you can erase something if it doesn't please you.

All prints, precolored or hand colored, must be sealed before cutting. Paint them with sealer solution in 3″-square segments and blot the sealer off immediately with Kleenex. Sealing prevents the colors from running and reinforces the paper for cutting and pasting.

CUTTING OUT YOUR PRINT

Materials

    Manicure scissors—good quality with fine, sharp, blades.
    Straight scissors to cut away excess paper.

Skillful cutting is a prime requisite for a fine piece of decoupage. First cut away all unnecessary paper for easier handling. If there are spindly tendrils or scrolls that might break off, draw "ladders" to nearby points to reinforce them. These ladders are cut off just before you are ready to paste.

If you are right-handed, hold the print in your left hand. Hold the manicure scissors in your right hand, with the curved blade pointing to the right and the palm of your right hand facing up, somewhat, as you cut. Feed the paper into the scissors with the left hand, turning it as you cut and wiggling it slightly. This creates a minute serrated and beveled edge, turned under, that adheres well when glued.

Cut inside spaces first so that there is more to hold on to while you're working. Poke a hole through from the top, then put the scissors up through the hole from the bottom to cut these areas; that way it's easier to see what you are doing. Eliminate unwanted details and backgrounds; silhouette the figures of the design.

Don't leave white edges or other evidence of inept scissoring. Very large prints should be cut into small segments, about 3″ square, and then reassembled when gluing. The extra cuts will let air bubbles and glue escape and aid drying. Judiciously placed, they will never be seen from a galloping horse, or under those 20 coats of varnish!

DECOUPAGE ON WOOD

MATERIALS FOR PREPARING BACKGROUND
> Plastic wood.
> No. 320 and No. 600 Tri-m-ite paper.
> Small sanding block.
> Sealer solution (half white shellac and half denatured alcohol).
> ½″ medium-quality brush (badger or ox-hair).

A simple wooden tray is a good beginning project. Choose a print of suitable size and style for the central motif. Some ornamental scrolls for the corners or a gold paper braid border to hold it all together might add interest, too. Gold braid requires three coats of sealer, dried after each coat, to protect it under varnish.

On new wood, fill any holes or scratches with plastic wood. Let this dry overnight. Sand the surfaces with the grain, using No. 320 Tri-m-ite paper. Remove any sharp corners or edges because they don't hold paint and varnish well, but don't make them rounded. Apply a coat of sealer, brushing it well into the grain and over the seams. Let it dry 30 minutes. Sand very lightly with No. 600 Tri-m-ite paper if there are rough spots.

If you are working on an old tray, first remove all of the old finish, then proceed as for new wood. Use a commercial finish remover, and follow the directions.

MATERIALS FOR PAINTING BACKGROUND
> Oil-base paint, satin finish, good quality, such as Sapolin, or Hiram Manning's, if available.
> Turpentine, artist's rectified, for thinning paint.
> 1″ good-quality ox-hair or badger brush.
> Oil paints in tubes for modifying color—cadmium yellow, ultramarine blue, alizarin crimson, raw umber, raw sienna, Venetian red, white, black.

Mix a color that harmonizes with the colors in your print. Paint the face of the tray in the morning and the back at night. Stand it on top of cans or jars to dry. Two coats are the minimum; you may need three or four. Wait 24 hours between each coat, longer in damp or rainy weather. Sand lightly with No. 600 Tri-m-ite paper. Seal the surfaces with sealer

solution and let them dry for 30 minutes.

There are many other ways to finish the background, employing such media as wood stain, gesso, gold leaf, marbleized papers and Chinese tea papers. Techniques for applying these can be found in the reference books following this Introduction.

GLUING

MATERIALS
> Mucilage for decoupage from Manning, Harrower or Mitchell. (These brands dry slowly and allow you to change your mind.)
> White glue, water soluble. (Sobo or Elmer's is a must for adhering gold braid; these dry clear, but fast—you *can't* change your mind.)
> Sponges, old bath towels, paper towels, Kleenex, wax paper.
> Roller or brayer, 3″ wide.
> Bowl of water.
> Paste brush, toothpicks, Q-Tips, corsage pin.
> Vinegar, to remove glue. (Use sparingly or you'll unstick everything.)
> Glycerin—one part glycerin to four parts Sobo will retard drying.
> X-acto knife.

Apply mucilage evenly and not too thickly all over the back of the print, or you may prefer to spread it over the surface where the print will be placed. Then rinse and dry your hands to prevent the print from sticking to your fingers and being torn.

Place the print on the tray, positioned accurately. Lay a hot, *well-wrung-out,* slightly damp piece of bath towel over it and roll with the brayer. Be careful not to slide the print out of position. Then press firmly but lightly from the center out with a barely damp sponge or small piece of towel. (Wring it out until it is almost dry.) Try to press out excess glue or air bubbles, rolling your fingers as you go. Be careful not to rub; this might damage your print or cause it to shift out of place. Press all edges down with your fingernail; hold the tray to the light to check on this. Anything that sticks up will cause trouble later when you varnish. Take care of it now.

Let the tray set for an hour or so and then, using a damp sponge or piece of towel (rinsed in hot water often and well wrung out), remove every bit of excess glue from the background and the top of the print. Allow to dry overnight. The next day check again for air bubbles. If you find any, slit them with an X-acto knife and apply glue. Probe all edges gently with the corsage pin and reglue them as necessary. Check for shiny spots; they are glue and must be removed because glue or mucilage turns brown under varnish. When all is perfection, apply a coat of sealer over the entire surface and let it dry overnight.

VARNISHING

MATERIALS

Varnish—4 oz. of good-quality semigloss, such as Hiram Manning's, Marie Mitchell's or McCloskey's.
Turpentine (artist's rectified).
Brush—½" or 1" ox-hair or badger, good-quality.
Tack cloth, to remove dust and lint between coats.
Tin cans—empty and all same height to stand tray on.
Brush cleaner.

Stir varnish gently but thoroughly before applying each coat. Don't shake the jar; it creates air bubbles. Work in a dust-free room, about 70°, never on a damp or rainy day or with the humidity above 54%. Flow the varnish on smoothly but generously; brush in opposite directions for each coat. Check for drips, accumulation on an edge, hairs and dust before and after each coat. Wait 24 hours after each coat; but you can apply one coat of varnish to the front in the morning and one to the back at night. The back of the tray needs only seven or eight coats. To test for dryness, press the surface with your finger; if it leaves any impression the varnish is not dry enough for another coat.

After 10 coats some *découpeurs* start to sand. You will be less likely to sand through the varnish and damage your print if you wait until you have applied 20. You may need even more coats than that if you wish to submerge the print completely. Wrap your brush in aluminum foil and keep it in the freezer between coats. When you're all finished varnishing, clean the brush in brush cleaner, wash it in heavy suds, rinse, shape and dry.

Other finishes for decoupage which you may wish to try, such as lacquers or acrylic polymers, are described in the reference books listed at the end of this Introduction.

SANDING

MATERIALS

No. 320, No. 400 and No. 600 Tri-m-ite paper.
Bowl of water and detergent suds.
Steel wool #0000.
Damp sponge and towel.
Small sanding block.
Goddard's wax.
Soft cloth.

Cut the Tri-m-ite paper into strips about 3" x 2" and mark the number (320, 400 or 600) on the back of each piece. Avoid the edges and corners of the tray until last or you may sand through and create a troublesome repair job. Dip a No. 320 strip into the suds and sand over the top of the design to reduce the surface down to the level of the varnish on the background. There will be a milky residue; wipe it off with a damp towel as needed. Don't sand all the way through to the print. If you do, touch up the spot with colored pencils to match, then with varnish on the tip of a brush. Apply five more coats of varnish, and be more watchful next time, especially on that spot.

Repeat the process with No. 400 Tri-m-ite over the whole face of the tray, taking down the varnish still more and obliterating any shiny spots. The sanding block may be useful here. Continue until the finish is uniformly smooth, and no edges of the print can be felt.

Repeat the process with No. 600 Tri-m-ite paper and it will now begin to have a polished look. A moiré shimmer may appear on the surface at some point in the sanding, but it will disappear subsequently. Now take about a 1" swatch of dry steel wool #0000 and polish the surface with a light, circular motion. Rub the edges of the tray with the steel wool, just enough to produce a soft satin finish. Polish with Goddard's wax and a soft cloth.

Let it rest for about a year, so that the varnish will cure and harden. Then it should be a joy forever as well as beautiful to behold!

BIBLIOGRAPHY

For inspiration and instruction in various other techniques and finishes to enhance your creations, the following books are recommended. The definitive text, by the master of us all, is that of Mr. Hiram Manning of Boston, Massachusetts—*Manning on Decoupage*.

Harrower, Dorothy, *Decoupage, a Limitless World in Decoration,* Crown Publishers, 1958. The first important book on decoupage to be published in the twentieth century describes decoupage and its antecedents, also collage and other related fields. Good reading.

Linsley, Leslie, *Decoupage, a New Look at an Old Craft,* Doubleday, 1972. Miss Linsley has concentrated on speeding up the procedures.

Manning, Hiram, *Manning on Decoupage,* Hearthside Press, 1969. The traditional method—blood, sweat and tears—but you'll have an heirloom, or a work of art, or both. Good reading, detailed instruction.

Mitchell, Marie, *Art of Decoupage* (manual), 1966, and *Advanced Decoupage* (manual), 1969. Clear and concise, follows traditional procedures.

Newman, Thelma R., *Contemporary Decoupage,* Crown, 1972. Covers history and traditional decoupage and has a whole chapter on decoupage on acrylic. Many innovations. Extensive sources of supply.

Nimocks, Patricia E., *Decoupage,* Scribner's, 1968. The chapters on coloring and cutting techniques are especially informative and helpful.

Sommer, Elyse, *Decoupage Old and New,* Watson Guptill, 1971. Mrs. Sommer appreciates fully the importance of traditional techniques and design in decoupage, but has stimulating new ideas, also. Good supply sources. Lesson plans for teachers.

Wing, Frances S., *Complete Book of Decoupage,* Coward McCann, 1965. Most of the emphasis is on the traditional approach. Mrs. Wing was among the first to recommend lacquer and plastic for speedy finishing and for objects receiving hard wear.

O'Neil, Isabel, *Art of the Painted Finish,* Morrow, 1971. A detailed study in this field, and a fine reference.

Grotz, George, *The Furniture Doctor,* Doubleday, 1962. Still a favorite of those who have restored or wish to restore a piece of furniture.

SOURCES OF SUPPLY

Adventures in Crafts, 218 E. 81st St., New York, N.Y. 10028. Instruction, wide selection of supplies. Mail order.

American Handicrafts Tandy Co., 1001 Foch St., Fort Worth, Texas 76110. Catalogue, supplies, mail order. Many branches all over the U. S.

Brandon Memorabilia, Inc., 3 W. 30th St., New York, N.Y. 10016. Gold braid, old prints, embossed prints. Mail order.

Connoisseur Studios, Inc. (Patricia Nimock's Decoupage) , P.O. Box 7187, Louisville, Ky. 40207. Good-quality prints, supplies.

Creative Crafts, 31 Art St., Ramsey, N.J. 07446. Bimonthly crafts magazine, new products, techniques.

Creative Workshop, 73 Cuttermill Rd., Great Neck, N.Y. 11021. Instruction and supplies.

Cunningham Art Supplies, Stone Mountain, Georgia 30083. Lacquer and its techniques, manual, materials and prints.

Dover Publications, Inc., 180 Varick St., New York, N.Y. 10014. Free catalogue; extensive pictorial archive of sixteenth- to twentieth-century illustrations. Mail order.

Harrower House, 37 Carpenter St., Box 502, Milford, N.J. 08848. Catalogue, prints, supplies and instruction by appointment.

The Manning Studio of Decoupage, 41 Upton St., Boston, Mass. 02118. Catalogue ($1.50), superb prints and supplies, instruction by appointment. Mail order.

Marie Mitchell's Decoupage Center, 16111 Mack Ave., Detroit, Mich. 48224. Manuals, prints, supplies and instruction. Excellent quality. Catalogue, mail order.

Morris Manufacturing Co., Inc., 3837 Dividend St., Garland, Texas 75042. Catalogue, prints, supplies, wooden boxes, purse fittings. Mail order.

O. P. Craft Co., Inc., 425 Warren St., Sandusky, Ohio 44870. Catalogue, boxes of all kinds. Mail order.

Hazel Pearson Handicrafts, Rosemead, Calif. 91770. Prints, supplies, catalogue, mail order.

J. C. Penney Co., Inc. Many stores all over U. S. Beginners kits, supplies.

Sears Roebuck and Co. Many stores throughout U. S. Kits, supplies, catalogue, mail order.

Singerie, 914 S. Robertson Blvd., Los Angeles, Calif. 90035. Prints, supplies, instruction. Catalogue, mail order.

Wicker World, 20651 Mack Ave., Grosse Pointe Woods, Mich. 48236. Basket purses of good quality.

Your own attic; also garage sales, thrift shops, junk shops and flea markets for unusual objects.

The National Guild of Decoupeurs, P.O. Box 5119, Grosse Pointe, Mich. 48236, requires that its members meet rigid standards of excellence and artistry in order to be accepted. If you become a dedicated *découpeur* you may wish to join.

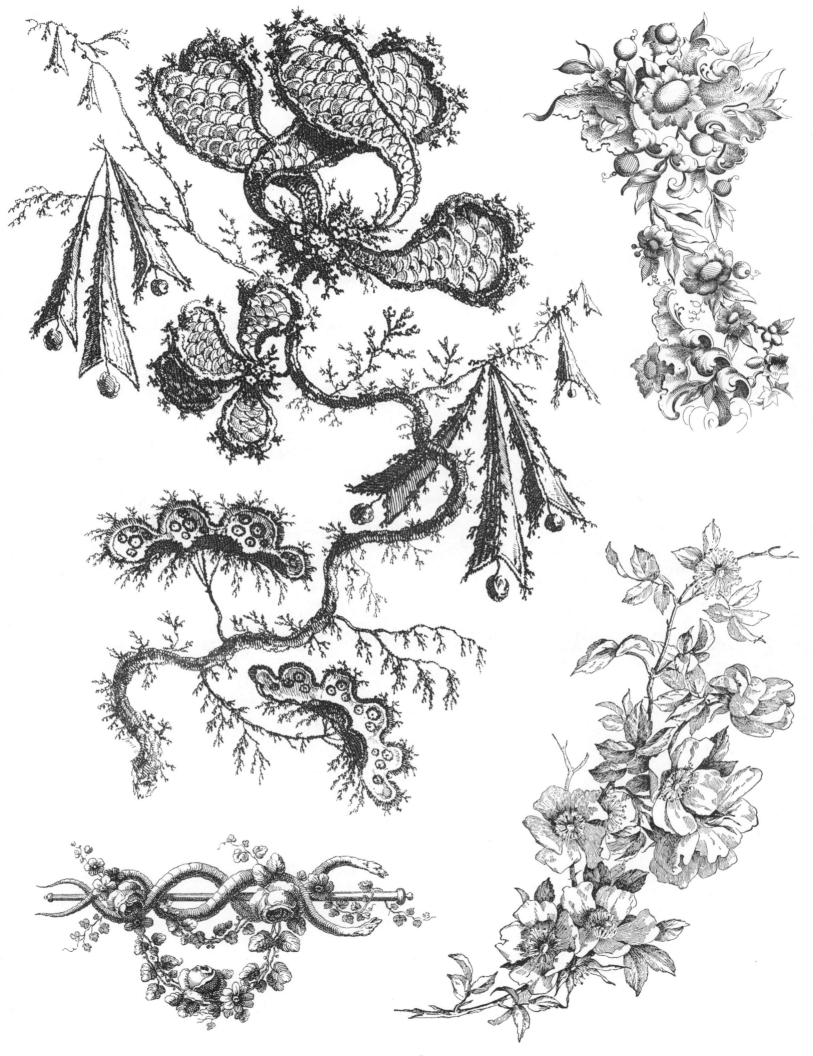

MDCCCL

14

BLOODROOT.

STAG-HORN SUMAC.

WILD GERANIUM.

SHINLEAF.

WILD ROSE.

GOLDENROD.

CHICORY.

YELLOW LADY'S-SLIPPER.

EARLY SAXIFRAGE.

TRUMPET-HONEYSUCKLE.

MARSH-MARIGOLD.

YELLOW ADDER'S-TONGUE.

POLLOCK'S CHARACTERS AND SCENES IN THE SLEEPING BEAUTY IN THE WOOD! OR, HARLEQUIN AND THE MAGIC HORN.

8 Pl. Characters 12 Pl. Scenes
4 Pl. Wings. Nº6 12.19.28 2 Pl. Tricks.

The Ogre Frosty Toes. London, Published by B. Pollock, 73, Hoxton Street Afterwards Clown Mr Harrison

A Book for the Above, Price 4

Prince Charming, Afterwards Harlequin, Mr Ambrook Princess Beauty, Afterwards Columbine, Miss C. Gibson Stapandfetchit, Afterwards Pantaloon

Columbine Harlequin Pub by E. SKELT Clown Harlequin Columbine

Pantaloon Clown Harlequin Clown Pantaloon

Relicf ART

L. Killer direxit

NDe Poilly ex.

J. Baptiste soul et ex cum priuil Regis.

22

Das Herz hüpft in der Bruſt, das leichte Füsgen ſpringet   So wohl beym Harfen Klang, als waũ die Leyer klinget.

31

33

E. Reiffer   F. Boucher inv   Prœdis APt.

37

43

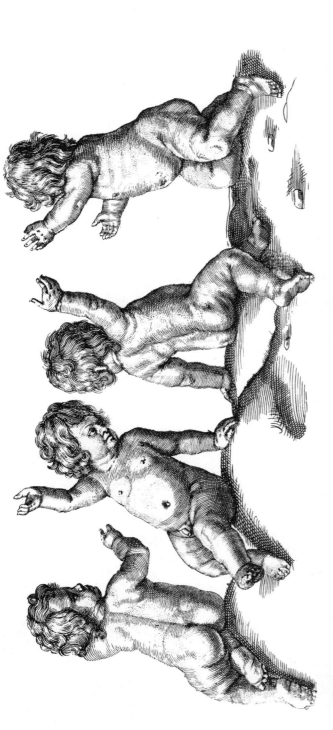

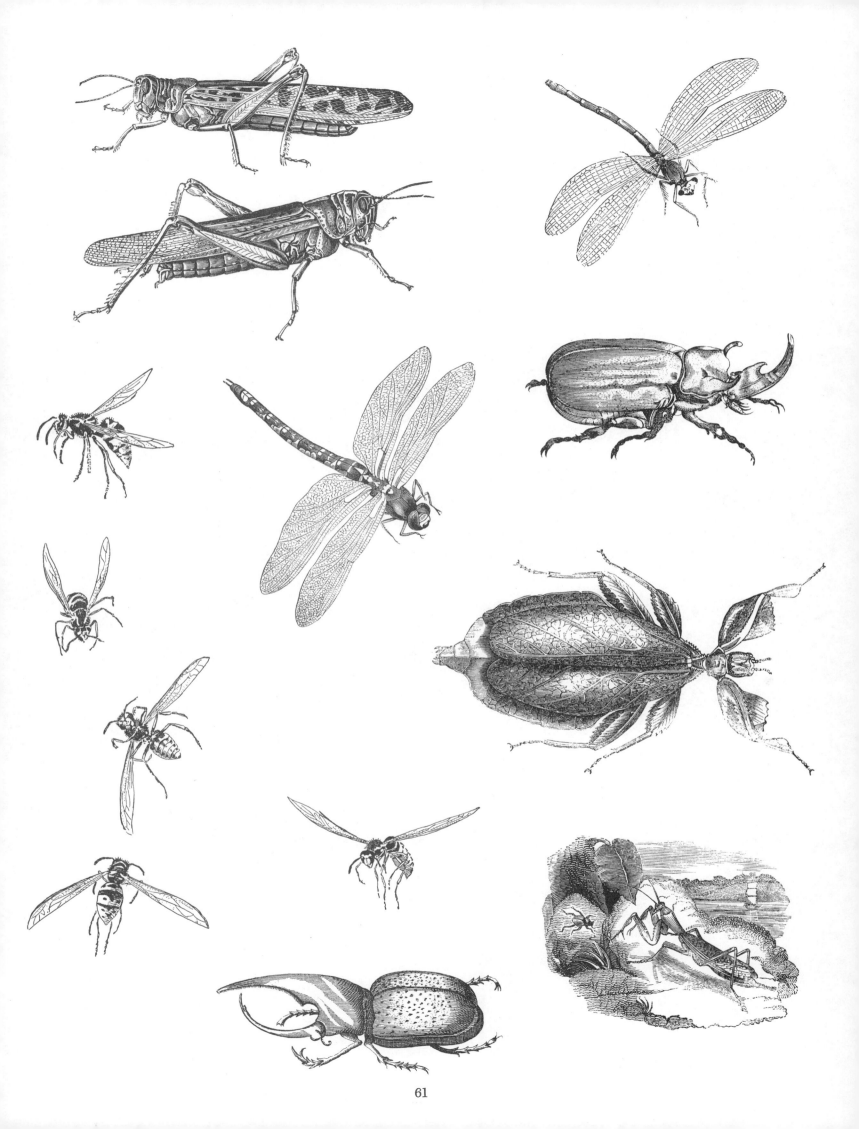

SOLI DEO GLORIA

FEAR GOD. & FEAR. NOUGHT.

Ton pour l'Appel.

Ton pour le premier Lancé.

Ton pour le Requêté ou Deffaut.

Ton pour l'Appel.

Ton pour le premier Lancé.

Ton pour le Requêté ou Deffaut.

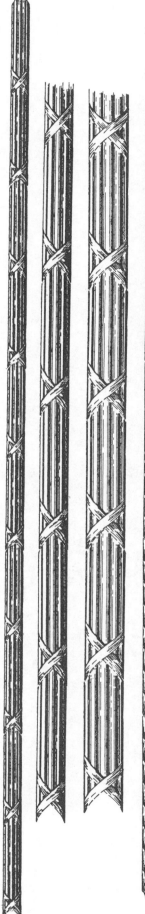
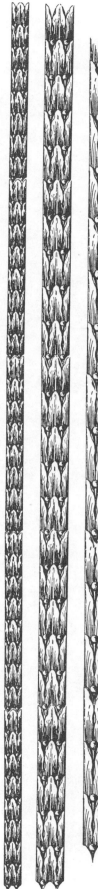

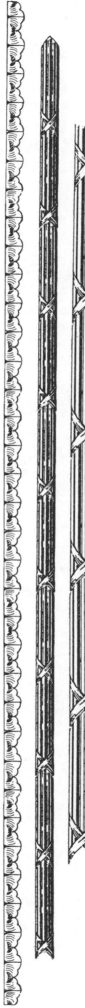
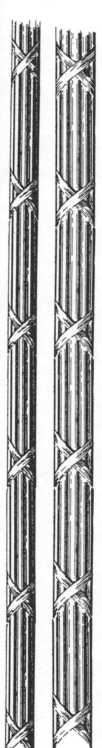
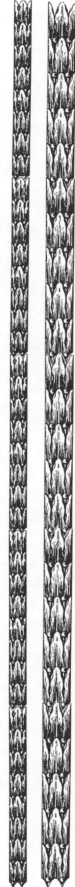

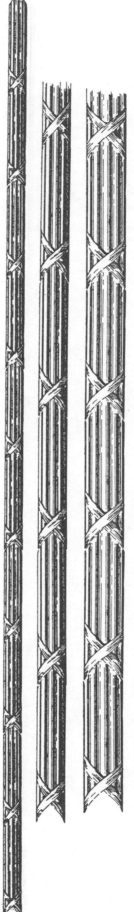

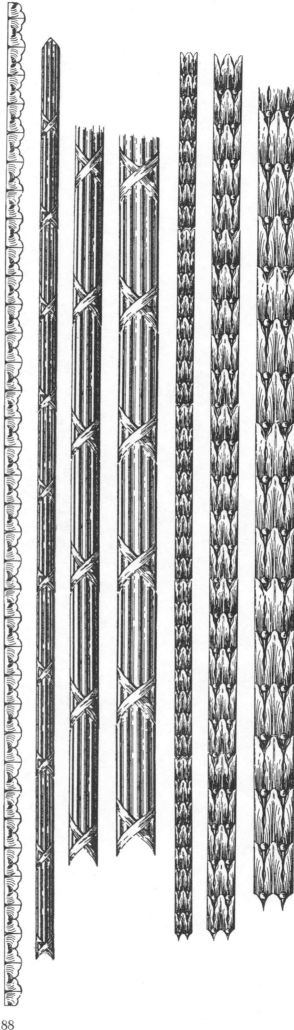

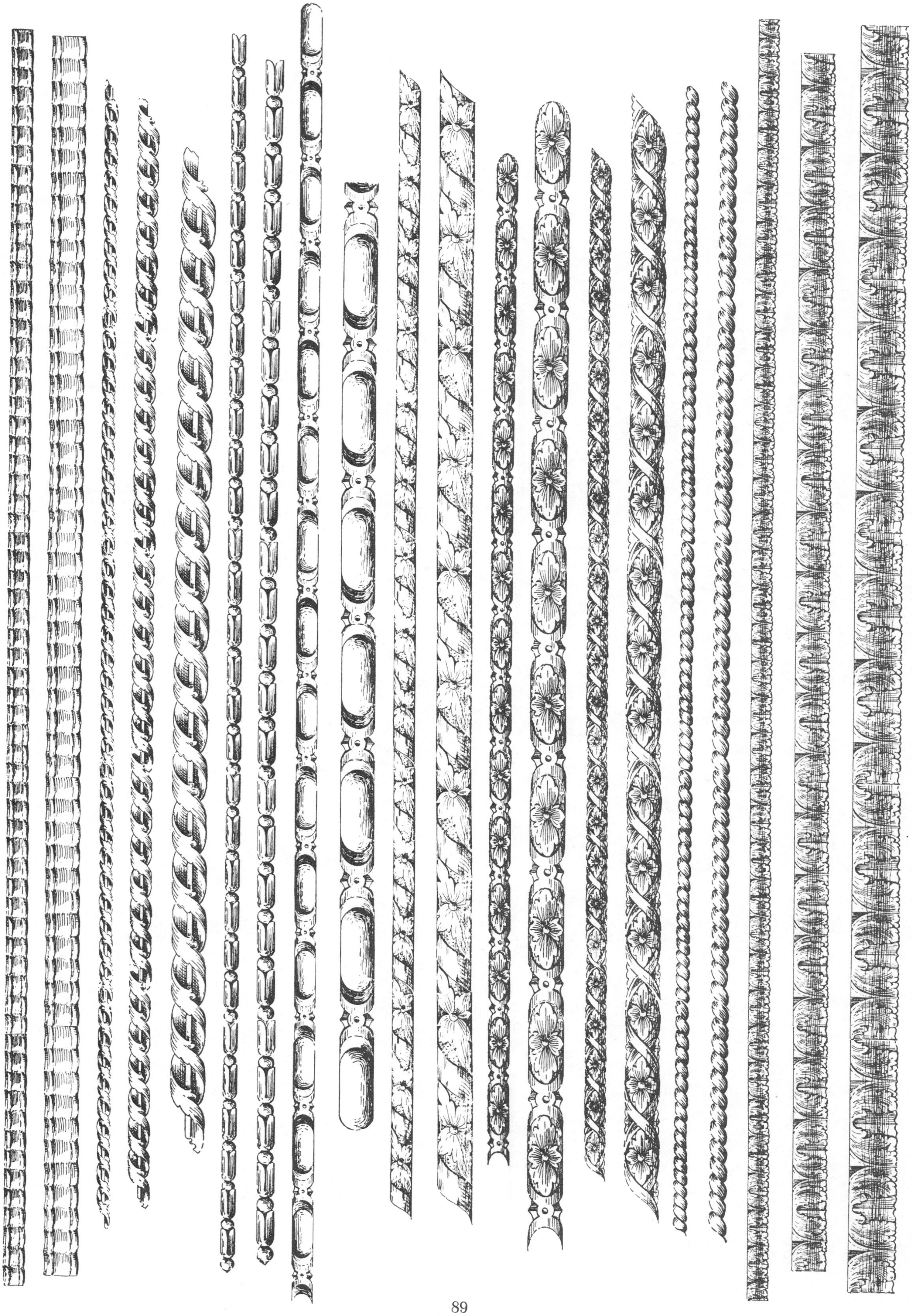

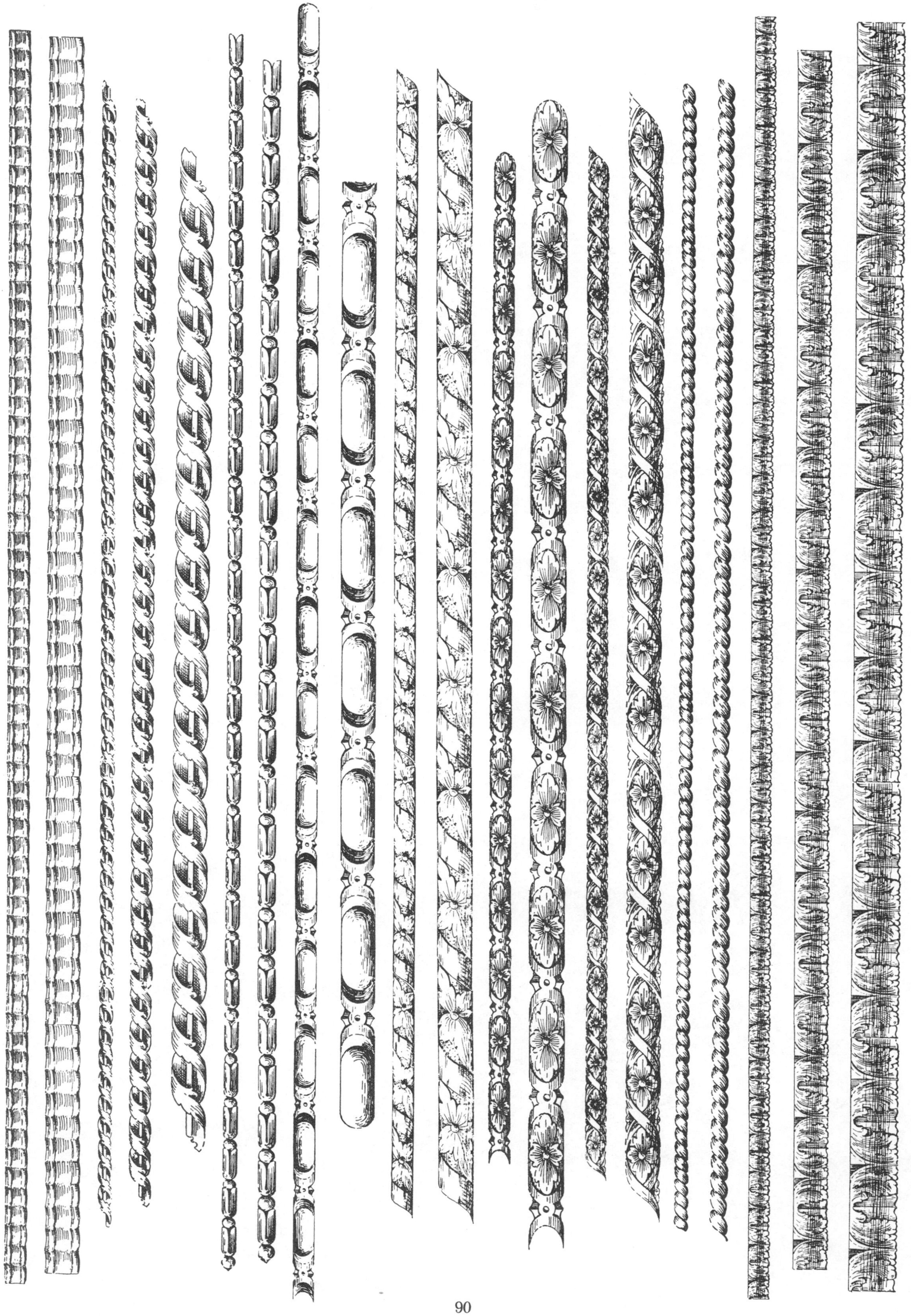

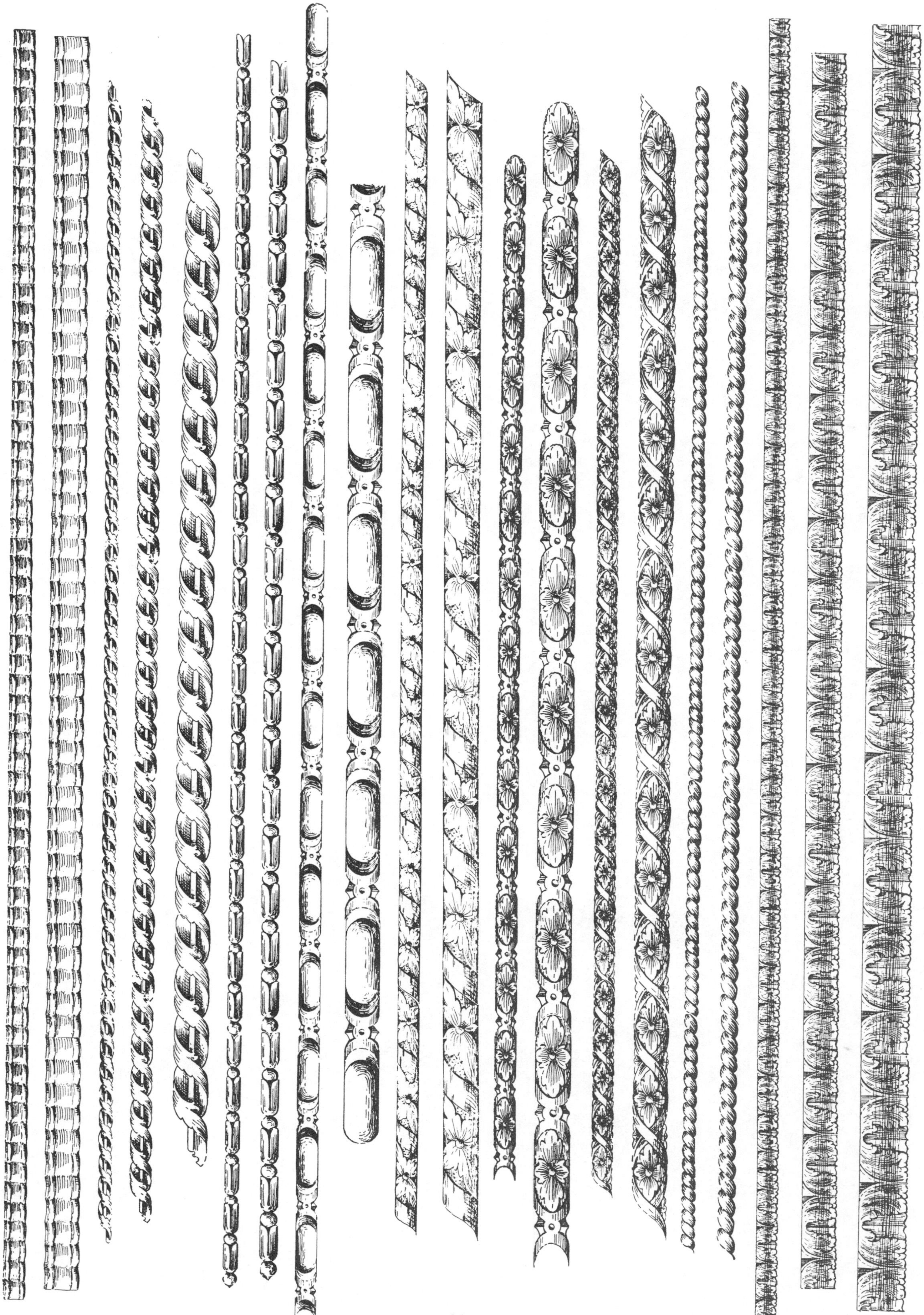

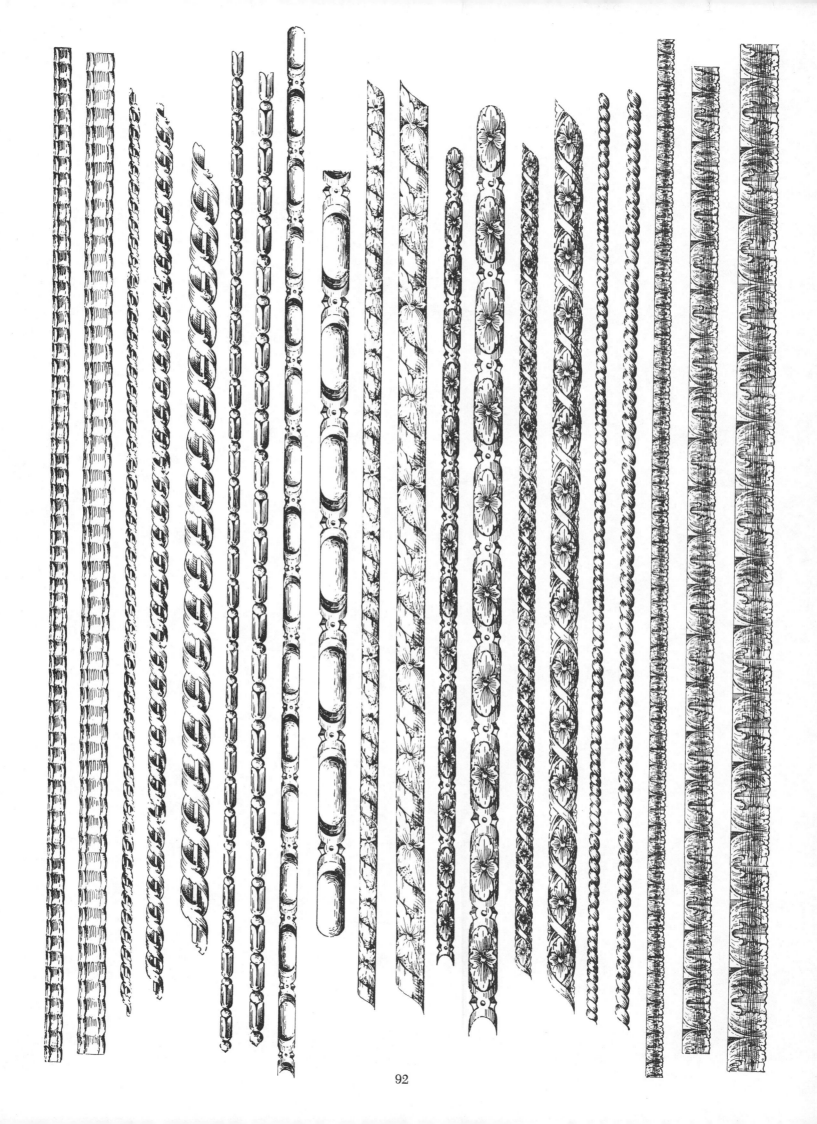